*John McCain*

John McCain in white boxer shorts, a T-shirt,
and black socks.

PLATE 1

Plate 2

Cindy McCain

Cindy McCain is wearing a contemporary
stretch knit slip-foundation garment.

John McCain wears formal "white tie and tails" for his wedding to Cindy Hensley (1980).

PLATE 3

Cindy McCain wears a retro-Victorian wedding gown
featuring a lace collar, lace lappets, mutton-chop sleeves,
and a full-length skirt accented with a satin band (1980).

PLATE 4

John McCain dons a traditional tuxedo for a
gala supporting Operation Smile, his wife's
favorite charity (2005).

PLATE 5

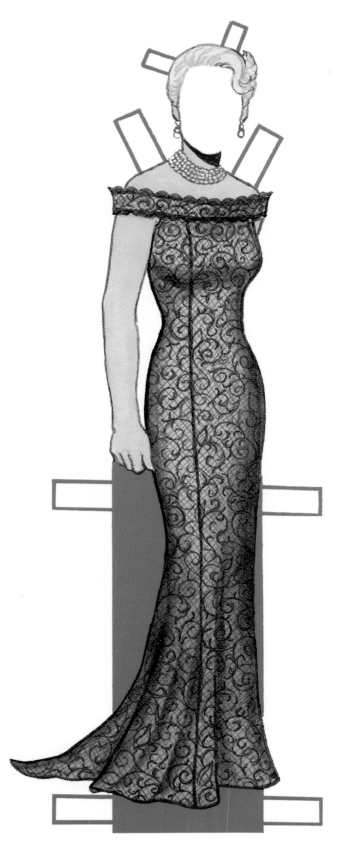

Cindy in a fitted full-length gown for an Operation Smile gala
(2005). The gown is black arabesque patterned net lace over
flesh-toned silk with a dropped portrait neckline.

PLATE 6

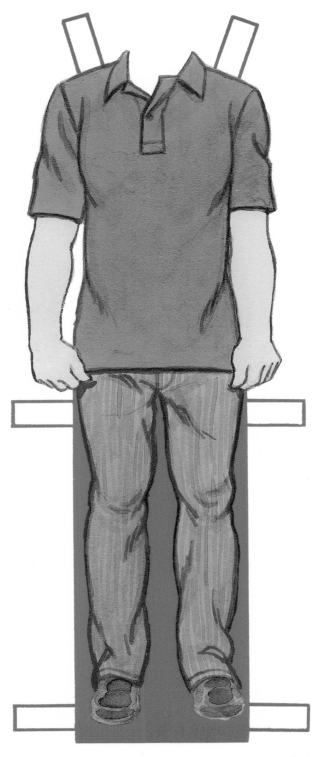

Senator McCain casually dressed in a turquoise knit
shirt and blue jeans during an informal visit with
George and Laura Bush (2005).

PLATE 7

For the Bush's informal visit (2005) Cindy wears a
white shirt and denim skirt. Her turquoise and silver necklace and
leather belt with silver trim give the ensemble a western look.

PLATE 8

PLATE 9

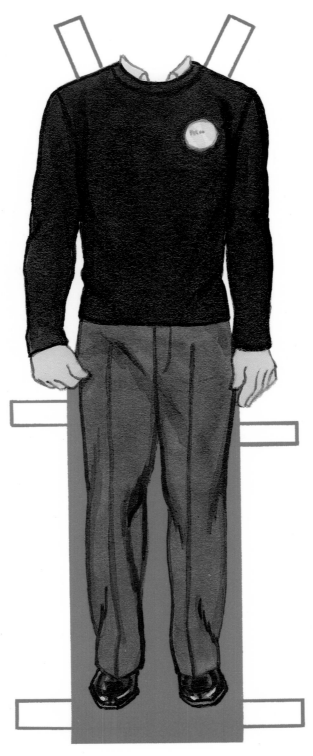

During informal campaign appearances, McCain often discards his jacket and greets the crowd wearing a sweater and slacks.

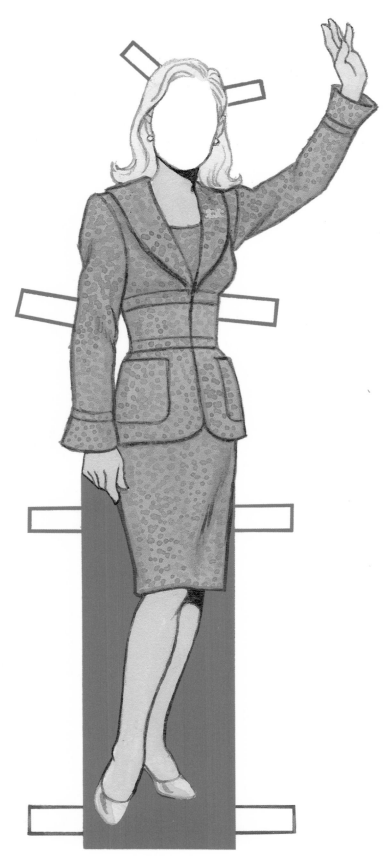

Cindy McCain wears a fitted suit of shocking pink slub wool
with a shawl collar and wide, flared cuffs on the jacket.

PLATE 10

John McCain dressed more casually when holding Town Hall meetings during his campaign for nomination. Here he wears a black business suit, a blue cardigan sweater and shirt with no tie.

PLATE 11

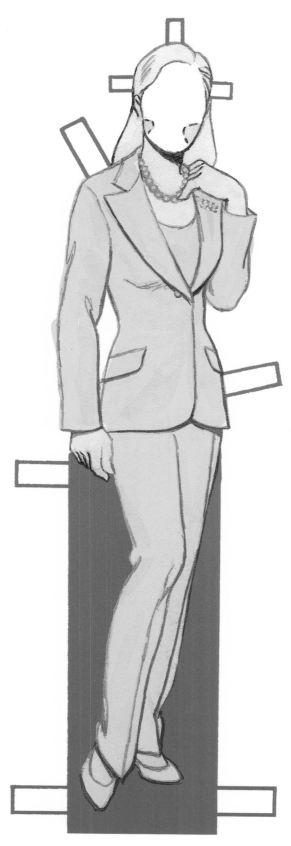

Cindy in a buttercup yellow slack suit with matching top for
an interview on *The Tonight Show with Jay Leno*.

PLATE 12

During a whirlwind tour of Europe and the Middle East, John McCain walks through an open market in Baghdad wearing a bulletproof vest for security reasons.

PLATE 13

Cindy McCain makes many campaign appearances by herself. Here she wears a navy blue-and-white tweed suit with a turtleneck sweater and black stockings.

PLATE 14

John McCain in a navy blue suit worn with a pale
blue shirt and striped blue tie.

PLATE 15

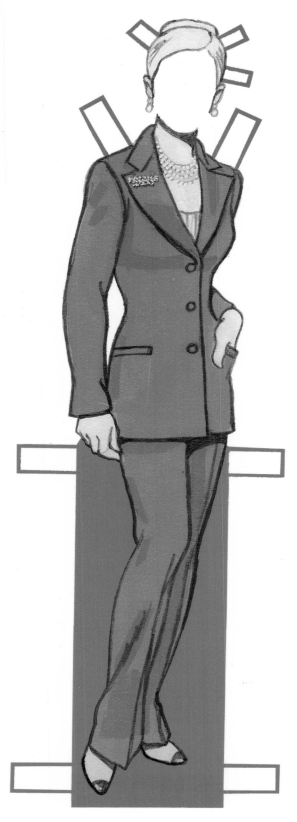

Cindy McCain campaigns in a bright red suit accessorized
with multi-strands of pearls, Chanel shoes, and a
rhinestone "McCain 2008" pin.

PLATE 16